WESTPRINT OUTBACK MAPS

an imprint of

meridian maps

AF867399

Binns Track

Revised 2nd Edition

• 4WD ADVENTURE GUIDE •

Digital versions of the Binns Track maps are available for download at:
www.meridianmaps.com.au/product/binns-track-digital

MAP SYMBOLS

Highway; Distance between major features	Watercourse; Waterhole; Fishing spot
Major road, sealed; Unsealed; Bridge	Perennial lake; Mainly dry or salt lake
Minor road, sealed; Unsealed; Minor distance	National or conservation park
Station track (private); Grid; 4WD track; Gate	Regional or other reserve
National highway; National route; State routes	Military or prohibited area (no access)
Homestead; Ruin; Landmark or tourist feature	Aboriginal land (permit may be required)
Pastoral Lease or Aboriginal Land boundary	Windmill; Yard; UHF Tower; Parking bay
Railway line and station	Rest area; Airstrip; Fuel; Accommodation
Bore or well; Spring; Tank or dam	Camping; Caravan park; All services

The ruins of Pedirka Siding on the Old Ghan Railway Line sit on an isolated, stony plain

The man and the story

Bill Binns has spent most of his life in the bush doing what he enjoyed most. His 32-year career with the Northern Territory Parks and Wildlife Service from the 1960s to 1990s shows his passion for wildlife and conservation. During his years travelling throughout the Territory he formed the view that there would be benefits from increased four wheel drive visitation from the southern states. He knew the Territory well and had driven all the stock routes, many abandoned since the 1960s. In 1993 Bill Binns contacted John Deckert from Westprint Maps to see if there was an interest in developing a map series highlighting the particular stock routes that could be used to link various parks and features of the Northern Territory. This resulted in a map which is now referred to by Westprint as the Original Binns Track map.

John and Bev Deckert travelled many of the routes marked by Bill as they did the ground research for a proposed series of maps to be produced for the NT Government by Westprint. Two years later the first map featuring the East Macdonald Ranges was launched in Alice Springs. Although this map was a successful start, a change of government shifted the focus on this project and only one map in the series was published. Behind-the-scenes work continued with the idea of linking tracks resulting in the promotion of several designated 4WD tracks featuring the Explorer Territory logo. This culminated in the eventual launch of the Binns Track in May 2008.

Thousands of experienced four-wheel drivers have enjoyed the amazing diversity of Northern Territory landscapes ranging from deserts to tropics with matching wildlife and vegetation. The Binns Track is made up of varying road surfaces from bitumen highways to rugged, tyre-punishing rocky tracks and is not to be taken lightly. Although it is a track that has a regular flow of traffic, a small convoy of two or three vehicles is recommended for increased safety.

Bill Binns has now retired but still takes a personal interest in one of the longest tracks in Australia, the 2,200 kilometre Binns Track.

Above: The first 'Explorer Territory' sign used to direct 4WD travellers through the Northern Territory Outback.
Left: Westprint's original Binns Track map.

The Binns Track takes travellers across a wide range of Northern Territory landscapes from Simpson Desert sand dunes to Savannah rangelands, a total distance of around 2,200 kilometres.

The track is named after Bill Binns who spent 32 years working as a ranger for NT Parks and Wildlife. Bill dreamt of a tourist route that took in many great sights, rock formations, native wildlife and the spectacular colours of Central Australia. The Binns Track is an acknowledgement of the work Bill Binns contributed toward this project.

Most sections can be travelled by 4WD and camper trailer, but Gregory National Park presents one of the most difficult landscapes in the Northern Territory for 4WD vehicles.

Some tracks are rocky with many sharp creek crossings suited only to high clearance vehicles. Camper trailers are not recommended and rigs with 50 mm towing balls may suffer significant damage.

Rocky ledges with 300 mm drops are not uncommon and vehicles with soft suspension and low towing hitches can expect difficulties. Crossing the Humbert River at Humbert Yard can be particularly challenging. Walk the rock ledges on the north side before driving.

The Broadarrow Track is recognized for having many sharp rocks and reports suggest that this track is particularly hard on tyres. Alternative routes for camper trailers are shown on these maps.

Above right: Old Police Station Waterhole in the Iytwelepenty/ Davenport Ranges National Park.
Below: Driving on a track across the Finke River floodplain.

1. Oodnadatta

An adaptation of an Aboriginal word meaning 'blossom of the mulga'. The explorer, John McDouall Stuart, named many local features during his first attempt to cross Australia in 1859. E M (Ned) Bagot was responsible for construction of 500 miles (800 kilometres) of telegraph line from Pt Augusta to the Macumba River at £50 a mile. Workers on the Overland Telegraph Line camped at nearby waterholes.

In 1874 John Forrest crossed the western half of the continent from Geraldton in Western Australia to the Telegraph Line about 30 kilometres north of the Angle Pole. (The Angle Pole is just north of Oodnadatta where the Overland Telegraph Line changed to a more northerly direction.) As he moved south towards what is now the Peake repeater station, Forrest camped at Angle Pole Waterhole where he blazed a tree and carved his initials and camp number.

Oodnadatta Township was surveyed in 1890 in preparation as a railhead on the Central Australia Railway. Good artesian water, found at 432 metres supplied 1.2 million litres a day for the railway and town which became the inland's most northerly service centre. Camel trains operated by Afghan Cameleers provided transport to outlying station properties and to Alice Springs from Oodnadatta. As many as 400 camels were based in the part of town known as Afghan Town.

The repeater station for the Overland Telegraph Line was eventually moved from Peake to Oodnadatta and the telegraph line gradually relocated beside the railway track. Some of the health, welfare and spiritual needs of the community were aided by the opening of an Australian Inland Mission hostel in 1911 by the Rev. John Flynn. He was later to become famous for the establishment of the Royal Flying Doctor Service. Oodnadatta's importance as a service centre lessened when the railway line was opened to Alice Springs in 1929, but the need for an airport, a meteorological station, railway and telegraph line repair crews, guaranteed its survival.

Angle Pole, Overland Telegraph Line

In 1980 the Ghan railway was realigned north from Tarcoola and appeared to sound the death knell for Oodnadatta, however a new breed of 4 wheel drive 'Ghan traveller' has helped the town change direction. The railway station has been restored and opened as a tourist centre and museum.

Oodnadatta's history is also its future and a few days exploring that history will be well rewarded. Facilities include: police station, hospital, public toilets, telephone, two general stores, fuel, water, hotel, meals, accommodation, minor mechanical repairs, museum and Caravan Park. For tourist information contact the Pink Roadhouse. Ph 08 8670 7822.

Overland Telegraph Line

Australia's lack of direct communication with any other part of the world led to a proposal to build a telegraph line that would connect Australia to Europe. In 1870 the South Australian government finalized negotiations with the British-Australian Telegraph Company to build a telegraph line across Australia to link with a submarine cable being laid under the sea from Java. Work commenced in September, 1870. Charles Todd, Postmaster General and Director of Telegraphs for South Australia, was in charge of the project that was due to be completed by January, 1872.

Meticulous planning enabled the southern sections to be completed on schedule but the unknown vagaries of the Top End wet season caused havoc and misery to all involved. Huge floods in the Katherine River halted construction and marooned work parties. Flooding of smaller rivers and creeks and tracks turning to mud caused parties to be split and isolated. Most of the men were weak or ill and many almost starved because supplies could not be moved. Fortunately, Ralph Milner was overlanding a large mob of sheep to Darwin and was also held up by floodwaters. As he neared the marooned construction workers a desperate effort was made to get some sheep through the flood waters to the men. This was the first substantial food the men had eaten for weeks.

The Roper River was used as a supply line for food and materials shipped to Roper Bar and ferried by small craft to the linesmen. The northern section of the line was eventually completed and both northern and southern sections joined at Frews Ponds in August 1872. The Overland Telegraph Line was one of Australia's great engineering feats.

Adam and Lynnie Platé put tremendous effort into attracting tourists to Oodnadatta and the Aboriginal community became involved in the town's survival. Adam and Lynnie arrived in Oodnadatta in 1974. By 1980 Adam had named the Oodnadatta Track and put up a massive sign on the Stuart Highway extolling the virtues of 'the track'. He and Lynnie started the Pink Roadhouse (pink paint was cheap) and Adam carted fuel and supplies to mining survey camps in the Simpson Desert. Adam also operated a regular supply freight truck between Adelaide and Oodnadatta. At the Pink Roadhouse he mended hundreds of 4WD tyres. His passion and advice for reliable tyres and correct tyre pressures for varying conditions was almost legendary amongst travellers in the outback. Adam and Lynnie developed a caravan park behind the roadhouse and everyone who has travelled the Oodnadatta Track knows of Adam's oil-drum-lid sign posts.

One of Adam's many passions was the Targa Rally. While competing during August 2012, Adam was killed when his car clipped a tree and slid about 70 metres down a hill. Adam's navigator, Patrick Chan walked from the vehicle. Not only Adam's wife Lynnie, his family and the people of Oodnadatta mourned his death but hundreds of people around Australia will remember the outspoken Legend of Outback South Australia. Lynnie sold her interest in Oodnadatta in early 2014 and moved to Adelaide ending an era that will be long remembered in Outback South Australia.

2. Macumba Station

The Macumba River was named by Stephen Jarvis in 1862. Jarvis used the Aboriginal name which means 'big fire'. According to Aboriginal mythology, the fire burned many trees in the river long before white man arrived. The station was taken up by J. Gilbert in 1872 and purchased by Sydney Kidman about 1919. In the past Macumba, together with Hamilton and Eringa were part of the vast chain of stations owned by Kidman. His plan was to form corridors across the nation and hopefully drought-proof his cattle empire. For further information read Kidman, the Forgotten King available from Westprint.

Dalhousie Spring

3. The Alberga River

During the construction of the Overland Telegraph Line in 1871 this part of the Alberga River was known as the Macumba River and signifies the division of the southern and central sections. The southern section was contracted to Ned Bagot, later involved in the establishment of Dalhousie Station near the Simpson Desert and Undoolya Station near Alice Springs (the first in the Northern Territory).

4. Fogarty's Claypan

Tom and Jess Fogarty managed the first Oodnadatta store as an extension to their existing business in Alice Springs and as this claypan forms part of the original route between Oodnadatta and Alice Springs, it is assumed that the claypan was named after them.

5. Mt Sarah Station

While exploring the route for the Overland Telegraph Line in 1871, John Ross named four mountains after his children. Mt Sarah, Mt Rebecca, Mt John and Mt Alexander are all in the same general area.

6. Hamilton station

A major cattle producing property. Follow the main track which leads across Hamilton Creek toward Eringa and Pedirka.

Pedirka Siding must have been one of the loneliest places on the line, built on a barren stony landscape seemingly isolated from the rest of the world. The Aboriginal meaning for Pedirka is 'hailstones'. Only ruins remain. Many of the creeks on the track to Dalhousie Springs are lined with gidgee trees (Acacia cambagei) and the red mulga or minnaritchie (Acacia cyperophylla). Red mulga has a distinctive red curling bark, sparse foliage and grows in creeks that cut across the stony tablelands. It was preferred for posts and building timber by station owners but few workmen would use its very hard wood. It grows in a very narrow band across Australia and is one of Australia's rare trees.

7. Dalhousie Homestead

Ned Bagot, contractor for the southern section of the Overland Telegraph Line, purchased the first lease of Dalhousie. He had previously set up Undoolya, the first cattle station in the Northern Territory, but lost heavily on investments in gold mining at Pine Creek. He sold these investments to buy Dalhousie.

Bloods Creek Waterhole

The first pastoral lease was taken up in 1872. During the following decade the Dalhousie homestead, yards and outbuildings were built. The large hill to the east of the homestead is called the Dalhousie Pile and is a series of extinct mound springs. On the Pile, about a kilometre from the homestead, some mounds of rocks can be seen to the west of the track. These rocks mark the boundary of the racetrack.

8. Dalhousie Springs

The springs were an important resource for Aborigines, providing water in abundance, shelter from the elements, valuable food and medicines. They managed to keep this wonderful valley of springs a secret from Stuart who came through this area in 1859. Alfred T Woods, an Overland Telegraph overseer and his men came across this great fracture zone in 1870. Christopher Giles wrote, 'We beheld a singular spectacle. The ground we had been traversing abruptly disappeared and we found ourselves on the brink of limestone cliffs 50 to 70 feet high'.

The party saw 'waving green reeds, with large pools of water at intervals, and dotted with island cones topped with reeds or acacia bushes'. These thermal springs were named Edith Springs after the wife of Sir James Fergusson, Governor of South Australia at that time. Lady Edith requested that the name be changed to honour her father the Marquis of Dalhousie.

9. Bloods Creek

Bloods Creek was named after JHS Blood, stationmaster at the Peake telegraph office in 1872. Two waterholes on the creek provided a good camping place for construction workers on the Overland Telegraph Line and continued to be used by travellers. A wine shanty and store was built nearby. Bloods Creek station was used for the breeding of Angora goats by the first long term occupiers who were early boring contractors named Bailes.

Ted Colson, who in 1936 became the first European to officially cross the Simpson Desert both ways, may have been the last occupier of Bloods Creek. Colson was an experienced bushman who had spent most of his life in the outback. As a youth he had walked, with his father, from Southern Cross to Coolgardie in the Western Australian goldfields. He later worked on the Overland Telegraph Line, searched for Lasseter's reef, and made several expeditions with prospectors, acting as guide and cameleer.

Colson, with 6 camels and an Aborigine from the Musgrave Ranges, took 12 days to cross from Bloods Creek to Birdsville and 16 to return. He named Alice Hills after his wife; Glen Joyce, after a friend's two daughters who died tragically; and Lake Tamblyn after his school master. Colson was 54 when he made the journey. Colson died in a level crossing accident in 1950, aged 68.

10. Eringa

In 1899 Sidney Kidman took up 2096 square miles (5428 square kilometres) of country in South Australia adjoining the Northern Territory border. He then stocked it with horses from Owen Springs and called the property Eringa. Although Eringa Waterhole was not permanent, Kidman was able most years to funnel stock from northern properties through Eringa to the rail head at Oodnadatta. This was the first property owned solely by Kidman. He named his home at Kapunda after the waterhole and station.

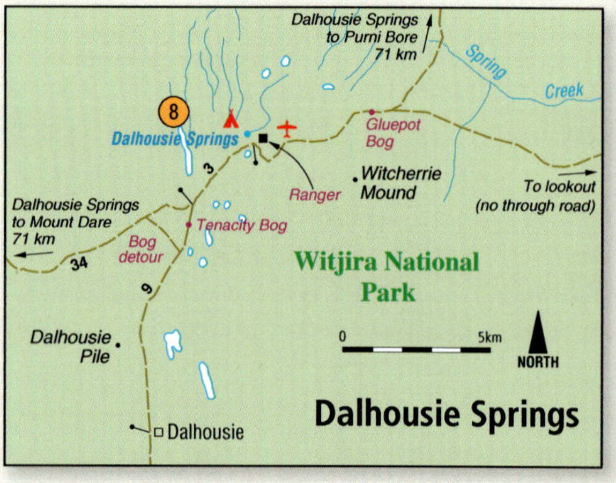

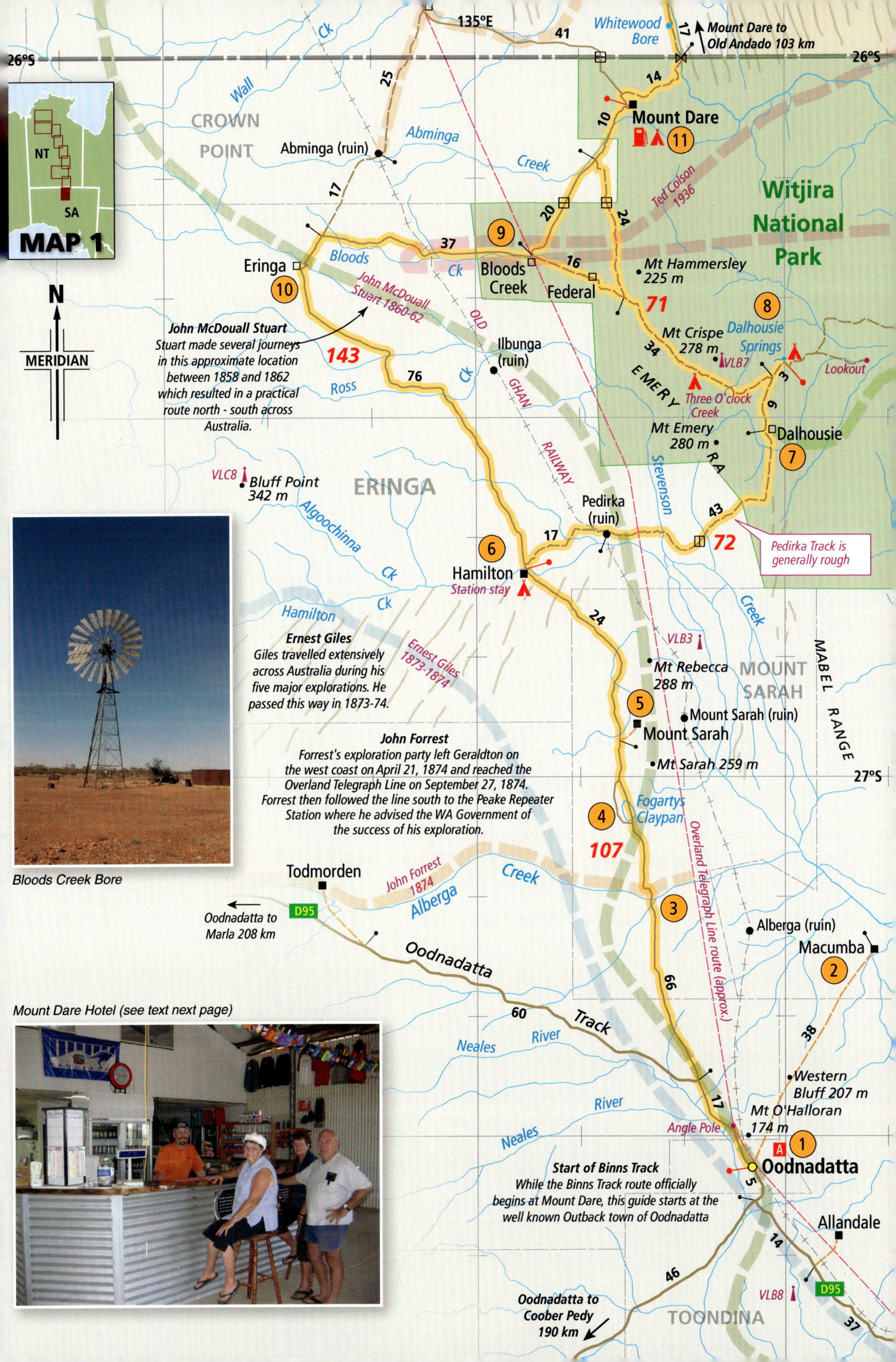

Bloods Creek Bore

Mount Dare Hotel (see text next page)

11. Mount Dare

Ned Bagot purchased the first lease of Dalhousie Station and built the homestead, yards and outbuildings. In later years a new homestead was built some distance away and named Mount Dare, after Mount Daer which is just across the border. Mt Daer is almost certainly named after an Overland Telegraph Line worker who was killed on the Roper River in the early 1870s.

Dalhousie Station was sold by Rex Lowe to the National Parks and Wildlife Service in 1984 and later dedicated as Witjira National Park. Phil and Rhonda Hellyer leased Mount Dare Homestead in the mid-1980s. They provided a service to travellers and Phil also re-opened the track between Mount Dare and Andado. A new hotel was built at Mt Dare in 2006. For information phone 08 8670 7835. For further information, see www.mtdare.com.au

12. Finke River

The Finke River was named by John McDouall Stuart in 1860 after his sponsor William Finke but known by Aborigines for centuries as Larapinta.

The Finke is claimed to be the world's oldest river because it has been running in its present course for longer than any other. Aerial photographs show that the Finke has cut its course through several mountain ranges. This signifies that the river was in place before the mountains started rising, allowing the river time to cut through the rock. As much of this rock is of the Precambrian period and is about 2000 million years old, the river must also be even older. Sixty thousand years ago the Finke River ran continuously, filling Lake Eyre to a depth and size much larger than today. Now it normally flows once or twice a year and not always throughout its full length.

Driving across the Finke River floodplain

The largest recorded flow was in 1974 when the Finke River ran for nine months. In that year much of Central Australia recorded rainfall of up to 1,000mm or 40 inches and Lake Eyre reached its highest recorded level. Even with that enormous flow of water, the South Australian Lands Department claim the Finke did not join with the Macumba to run into Lake Eyre. Water from the Finke River soaked away in the gigantic flood plain along the south western edge of the Simpson Desert.

Old Andado Homestead

13. Old Andado

The Simpson Desert covers a large portion of the south eastern section of the Northern Territory. Andado is the largest station and is located further into the desert than any other. Andado, at 10,859 square kilometres is the third largest single station in the Territory, about 2000 square kilometres smaller than Wave Hill and Brunette Downs.

Old Andado Homestead is about 20 kilometres within the Simpson Desert, and was built by the McDill brothers, who were the first lessees, taking up the property in 1909. They slept under the stars until 1922 when George McDill married and built the homestead.

At one stage McDills ran 6000 sheep, doing their own shearing and scouring the wool. Eventually sheep gave way to cattle just as drovers gave way to road trains. The present owners only run cattle.

Molly Clark grew up in South Australia and trained as a nurse in Adelaide. Illness forced her to abandon her career and she eventually went to Mungerannie Station on the Birdsville Track to work as a governess.

In 1946 she married Mac Clark and moved to Lake Harry Station which they managed until it was sold several years later. Other managing positions on stations in the Northern Territory followed. In 1955 they were offered a partnership in Andado, with the possibility of purchasing the property at a later stage.

Mac Clark Waddi (Acacia peuce) trees

"As we had three sons, we thought this a good opportunity. Long hours, much hard work, and years later we began to see that it might all come to fruition; we had even weathered the eight year drought without being too far in the red. A new homestead had been built by 1955, as now the old one of 1922 bush timber and iron could not cope with the expansion of work and staff necessary," said Mrs. Clark.

By 1970 they formed a family partnership so their teenage sons could participate. Things went well until 1978 when tragedy struck. Mac suffered a heart attack and died after his plane crashed on the property some distance from the homestead.

Molly's eldest son took over management of the property, working around the clock with few staff to try to clear remaining debts. Ten months later, while returning from Adelaide in a stock truck, he was killed in a level crossing accident.

Molly chose to battle on but at that time the Government forced her to completely destock her land as part of the tuberculosis and brucellosis eradication program. Because of the size and terrain of the property and the requirement that it be free of stock for three years, the cost of carrying out these orders was just too great. After the Government had finished shooting all their stock, they, like owners of many other properties were forced out of business.

Mrs Clark said, "But then how does anyone sell a place with no stock, restricted grazing area, and already showing signs of becoming dry. We bought some bulls and 2000 head of old cows and calves but it took us over two years to sell. We received a fair price but it left us with practically nothing. So much for 40 years' hard work and isolated living conditions."

Back in 1969 Molly had started to restore the old homestead for tourism. During the sale of the property she negotiated an agreement with the new owner to keep the old home and continue the restoration of an authentic 1920s station homestead.

In the mid-1990s Molly realised an ambition to promote recognition of Australian pioneer women by founding the National Pioneer Women's Hall of Fame. Molly believed that pioneer women were usually overshadowed by the exploits of men and she knew from practical experience that women contributed a huge amount toward the development of this nation.

The Pioneer Women's Hall of Fame has its base in Alice Springs. Molly passed away in 2012 passing her legacy onto her five grandchildren. In 2013 the Old Andado Charitable Trust was formed to maintain and restore this unique piece of Australia's history.

Old Andado Homestead is open to the public from March to October and there is an adjacent camping area with toilets and shower. There is an honesty box for camp fees and amenities are maintained by volunteer caretakers. For more information see oldandado.com.au or Old Andado Facebook pages.

14. Mac Clark Acacia Peuce Reserve

This reserve was named in honour of Mac Clark whose interest in these strange trees aided their survival. The Acacia peuce, also known as 'waddi' tree is thought to be a remnant of the last ice age. The wood is very hard and its foliage is quite prickly, especially when the tree is small. The adult tree usually has straight trunks, can grow 13 to 17 metres high and has large flat seed pods with seeds from 5mm to 10mm in diameter.

Three stands of these trees are known to exist in Australia. The largest at Boulia covers an area of about 100 square kilometres. Another is at Birdsville and the smallest at Andado where about 1000 mature trees are scattered over 10 square kilometres. Growth of young trees is slow and may only be 30 centimetres a year. Growth occurs after good rainfall and may almost stop during drought. It is not unreasonable to estimate that these trees are very old, possibly in excess of 500 years.

Until recently Acacia peuce had been eagerly sought for fence posts and building timber despite the hardness of the wood but their rarity has now been recognised and efforts made to protect them. This particular stand has a number of small trees. Acacia peuce only regenerates after exceptionally heavy rains and the only known periods of regeneration are following the floods of 1974 and 2010. Some seeds are being propagated in nurseries in an attempt to ensure the survival of this species.

C.T. Madigan is a well-known Australian explorer responsible for organising a scientific expedition to explore the Simpson Desert. He began planning about 1935 and spent the next few years developing a strategy to enable a successful crossing to be made. Much of his equipment was railed to Abminga, the most northerly rail siding in S.A., from where it was shifted in one of Harry Ding's trucks to Andado Station, via Charlotte Waters.

Tom Kruse, in later years famous as the Birdsville mailman, was in charge of the truck. Madigan's party left Andado early in July 1939, heading northward past the Acacia peuce trees and on over the gibber country to the junction of the Todd and Hale Rivers. Although this was not the first crossing of the Desert, it was possibly the most important as far as scientific research is concerned.

15. Simpson Desert

The Old Andado Track follows a corridor between two sand hills. This corridor is typical of the Simpson Desert where it is said that one can travel 400 kilometres without seeing anything but a dune on either side. The dune formation and vegetation is typical of the western half of the desert.

Driving along the Old Andado Track

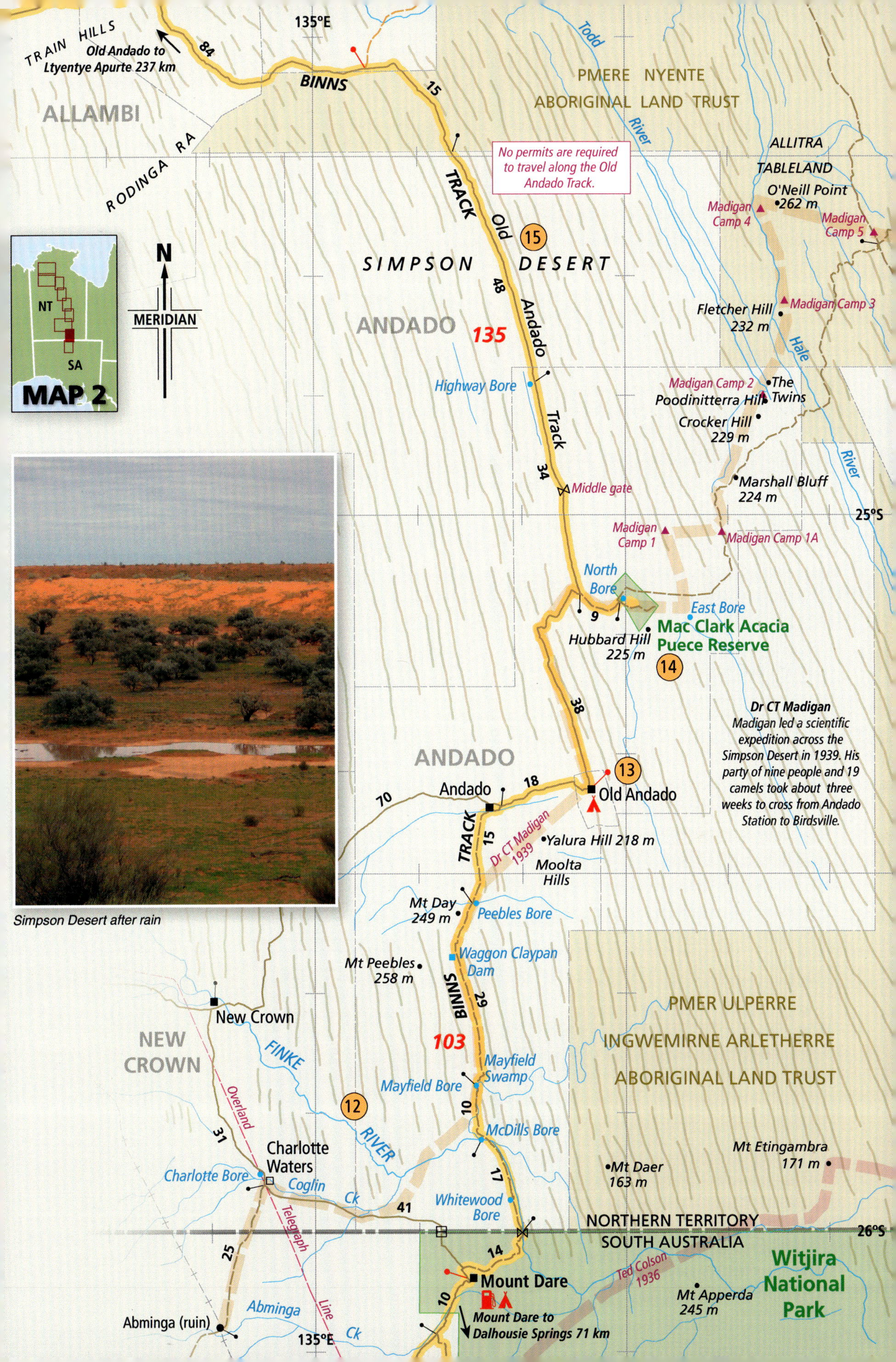

Simpson Desert after rain

16. Ltyentye Apurte (Santa Teresa)

The Catholic church showed an interest in establishing a mission for local Arrernte Aborigines about 1929 but it was not until 1939 that Father Moloney was able to start the Little Flower Aboriginal Mission near the Charles River north of Alice Springs.

By 1942 Alice Springs was an important military centre and it became necessary to move the mission. The authorities made the old mining town of Arltunga available but the problem of providing for about 400 people in an area unsuited to the task eventually led to the establishment in 1953 of Santa Teresa in an area closer to Alice Springs. The community now has a population of about 550 people.

Santa Teresa has an area of good pastoral country watered with bores and springs and well suited to cattle. New houses were built from local stone in a style slightly reminiscent of mission architecture in New Mexico. However, the new housing created a rift between Aboriginal custom and European expectation.

In Aboriginal culture it is customary to cease using a dwelling when the occupier dies. There is no problem with shelters built of leaves and twigs but with the permanent nature of new buildings at Santa Teresa this could not be allowed to happen. After conference with Aboriginal elders it was decided to compromise by allowing the immediate family of the deceased to exchange houses with another family, thus satisfying tribal law and yet ensuring the continued use of valuable dwellings.

The Aboriginal community is now responsible for the administration of their own land. The Aboriginal council appointed an officer and asked members of the Catholic Church to assist with community matters. People wishing to enter Santa Teresa must first contact the Administrative Officer during business hours.

17. Alice Springs

A major regional centre providing a service to the mining industry, cattle and pastoral interests and numerous outlying Aboriginal communities. For more information about the modern city please see the Westprint Tourist Guide for Alice Springs and Region.

18. Yeperenye (Emily and Jessie Gaps)

It was believed that the gaps were named during the construction of the Overland Telegraph Line in honour of the daughters of Charles Todd, Postmaster General and Director of Telegraphs for South Australia, who was in charge of the project. This was later found to be incorrect and the origins of the names Emily and Jessie is not known. In 1946 Emily Gap was the location for filming of 'The Overlanders' starring Chips Rafferty and Daphne Campbell. Aboriginal paintings can be found on the eastern wall of Emily Gap. In Aboriginal Dreamtime these gaps were associated with the Caterpillar Dreaming.

19. N'Dhala Gorge

This gorge is noted for its spectacular scenery and Aboriginal rock carvings. More than 5,900 petroglyphs and other culturally significant sites are located in the Gorge surrounds. The petroglyphs, many of which can be easily found on rocks near the 1.5km walking track, consist of two types – pecked and pounded and it is thought that this may represent two distinct time periods. The track from Ross River to the Ringwood road is recommended for 4WD vehicles only as it receives little maintenance.

Engravings at N'Dahla Gorge

Ross River Resort is based around the original Loves Creek homestead built in the 1890s as an outstation of Undoolya Station. Initially the outstation supplied fresh vegetables to the nearby goldmining community at Arltunga and later developed a reputation for breeding quality stock horses. Ross River Resort has a range of accommodation available. Ph. 08 8956 9711. www.rossriverresort.com.au

20. Arltunga Historic Reserve

After reports of valuable gem finds in 1886 about

200 prospectors rushed to the ruby fields at Ruby Gap and Glen Annie. Although these gems were found to be of little value, they brought experienced prospectors from South Australian goldfields who recognised the gold bearing possibilities of the Arltunga area. The first traces of gold were found in the creek beds around Paddy's Rockhole in April 1887 and miners soon found the first reefs.

Permanent water was a constant problem. Arltunga was not a rich field but it struggled along until the closure of the Government Battery in 1916. The population continued to decline to about 25 people in 1933.

A Catholic mission for Aborigines was located to the north of Alice Springs prior to the Second World War but when thousands were evacuated from Darwin to Alice Springs following air raids on Darwin and Meningitis reported within Alice Springs, an order was given to evacuate the mission to the old mining site at Arltunga. Although much work went into making the site suitable as a permanent mission it was constantly plagued by an unreliable water supply and was eventually moved to Santa Teresa in 1953. Hale River Homestead has a range of accommodation nearby. Ph. 08 8956 9993, www.haleriverhomestead.com.au

Ruby Gap

21. Ruby Gap Nature Park

This park has some of the most beautiful gorges found anywhere in Central Australia and even the most amateur geologist can find interesting geological formations along the cliffs that line the Hale River. In 1886, explorer David Lindsay was employed to survey this area and found gem sands showing traces of tin, garnets and brilliant red stones he believed were rubies at the entrance to a 'wild and romantic gorge' which he named Glen Annie, after his wife.

Eighteen months later there were 200 men in the Ruby Gap and Glen Annie areas but their dreams of fortune were soon dashed when it was discovered that the 'rubies' were garnets of little value. The great 'ruby rush' was the first mineral discovery in Central Australia which indirectly led to the discovery of gold at Arltunga and influenced the establishment of the town of Stuart, later known as Alice Springs, in 1888.

22. The Garden Station

A public road and a track to the Winnecke mines runs through The Garden Station. No access to other areas or tracks. The Turner family came to Arltunga to find gold but instead established a vegetable garden to supply the Arltunga and Winnecke gold fields. In 1921 James Turner leased an area around the garden and despite difficulty in finding permanent water, managed to establish a fine property. The Garden Station is now owned and run by the Hayes family.

23. Winnecke Gold Mines

Gold was found in 1902 by John McNeil at a point about six kilometres south of a soakage in the Hale River where explorer Charles Winnecke established a depot in 1894. Winnecke directed a survey by the Horn Scientific Expedition along the Finke River and through the MacDonnell Ranges. Perhaps one of the most valuable legacies of this expedition was the meeting of a party member, Professor Baldwin Spencer of the University of Melbourne, with Francis Gillen, postmaster at Alice Springs.

These two men became firm friends and their published research of the Aborigines of Central Australia is of immense anthropological value. The Winnecke Goldfield was based mostly on optimism but the growth of the field was not sustained by production. Most of the miners left in 1904 with a few battling on until 1916 when all activity ceased.

24. The Pinnacles Track

This track, recommended for 4WD only, was used for many years as a stock route and the bores along it are reminders of this period. It is now an infrequently used track with good scenery and, at the northern end, access to sections of the Harts Range Gem Fields.

25. Mud Tank Bore

Located on the intersection of the Pinnacles Track and the Plenty Highway, this area is well known to gem fossickers who frequent the zircon field about 10 km south. A maze of short tracks leads from the Pinnacles Track to an area known as Specimen Hill. Information can be obtained from the Gemtree Caravan Park.

26. Gemtree Caravan Park

A range of accommodation is available. A general store has food, diesel and ULP available. The Gem Room and Gallery have an extensive range of gems, jewellery and Aboriginal Art. New fossickers are especially welcome. A gem-cutter provides an on-site-service. Ph. 08 8956 9855. www.gemtree.com.au.

27. Harts Range Police Station

Located around 225 kilometres from Alice Springs, this station appears to be totally isolated from all habitation and even appears unnecessary. In fact it is possibly the largest two-man police district in the world. Police control an area of 110,000 square kilometres including 28 station properties and 15 Aboriginal communities with a total population of about 2000 people.

It can take five to six hours to reach a vehicle accident or emergency on the edge of their region. The Atitjere Community Store, to the east of the police station, has fuel, food, phone, camping and an ablution block. Ph. 08 8956 9773.

28. The Plenty Highway

A good bitumen road leading from the Stuart Highway can give one a false impression of an easy trip to Boulia. However this bitumen road will revert into a well-formed beef road, constructed in the early 1970s. Beef roads were built in the territory to improve the movement of cattle and boost the industry.

On reaching the Queensland border the road detiorates dramatically and is often only suited to 4WDs. A section of the O'Donohue Highway, between the border and Glenormiston Station can be particularly difficult during wet weather.

29. The Cattlewater Pass Track

This track was opened to the public early in 1994. It has been used for the movement of stock and supplies between stations since the late 1800s. Due to inconsiderate tourist use it is now closed.

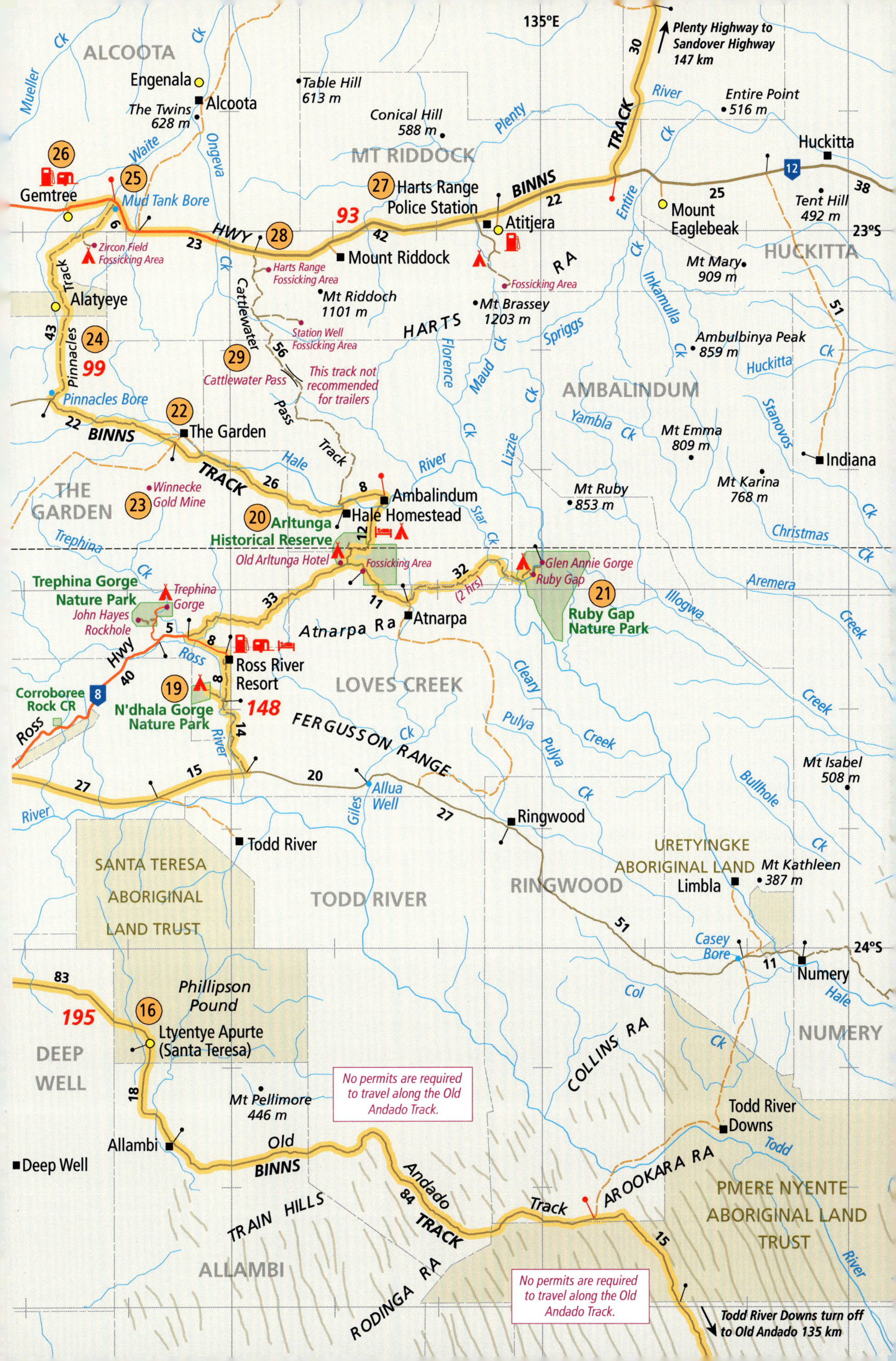
135°E
Plenty Highway to Sandover Highway 147 km
ALCOOTA
Engenala
Alcoota
The Twins 628 m
Table Hill 613 m
Conical Hill 588 m
MT RIDDOCK
Entire Point 516 m
Huckitta
26
Gemtree
25
Mud Tank Bore
Waite
Ongeva
Mueller
Plenty
River
27
Harts Range Police Station
93
BINNS
TRACK
30
22
Atitjera
Mount Eaglebeak
Tent Hill 492 m
38
12
23°S
HUCKITTA
Zircon Field Fossicking Area
23
HWY
28
42
Mount Riddock
Harts Range Fossicking Area
RA
Fossicking Area
Mt Mary 909 m
Alatyeye
Mt Riddoch 1101 m
Mt Brassey 1203 m
Inkamulla
51
Cattlewater
Station Well Fossicking Area
HARTS
Spriggs
Ambulbinya Peak 859 m
43
Pinnacles
24
99
29
Cattlewater Pass
56
This track not recommended for trailers
Florence
Maud
Huckitta
Ck
AMBALINDUM
Pinnacles Bore
22
The Garden
Pass
Yambla
Stanovos
BINNS
Track
Mt Emma 809 m
Indiana
Hale
River
Lizzie
THE GARDEN
Winnecke Gold Mine
23
TRACK
26
8
Ambalindum
Mt Ruby 853 m
Mt Karina 768 m
20
Arltunga Historical Reserve
Hale Homestead
Star
Christmas
Trephina
12
Old Arltunga Hotel
Fossicking Area
Glen Annie Gorge
Ruby Gap
Aremera
Trephina Gorge Nature Park
Trephina Gorge
32
(2 hrs)
21
Ruby Gap Nature Park
Illogwa
John Hayes Rockhole
33
11
Atnarpa
Atnarpa Ra
5
8
Ross River Resort
Creek
HWY
Ross
40
LOVES CREEK
Cleary
Corroboree Rock CR
8
19
N'dhala Gorge Nature Park
148
FERGUSSON RANGE
Pulya
Creek
Ross
River
14
Mt Isabel 508 m
Bullhole
27
15
20
Allua Well
Giles
Ringwood
River
Todd River
URETYINGKE ABORIGINAL LAND
Mt Kathleen 387 m
Limbla
SANTA TERESA ABORIGINAL LAND TRUST
TODD RIVER
RINGWOOD
51
Casey Bore
11
Numery
24°S
83
Phillipson Pound
Col
Hale
195
16
Ltyentye Apurte (Santa Teresa)
COLLINS RA
NUMERY
DEEP WELL
No permits are required to travel along the Old Andado Track.
18
Mt Pellimore 446 m
Todd River Downs
Allambi
Old
Todd
Deep Well
BINNS
Andado
AROOKARA RA
PMERE NYENTE ABORIGINAL LAND TRUST
TRAIN HILLS
84
Track
TRACK
15
ALLAMBI
River
RODINGA RA
No permits are required to travel along the Old Andado Track.
Todd River Downs turn off to Old Andado 135 km

30. Boxhole Meteorite Crater

The crater is located near Dneiper homestead and travellers need permission to enter. The crater is about 170 metres in diameter and 15 metres deep. It was formed by a nickel/iron meteorite thought to have hit the earth about 5,400,000 years ago. The meteorite exploded on impact scattering fragments for a distance of several kilometres.

31. Charles and Cora Chalmers

Charles Chalmers was a school teacher at Mungindi in New South Wales who dreamed of being a farmer. During the early 1920s he applied to the Northern Territory Government to lease land to the north east of Alice Springs. His knowledge of this land was from a school atlas which showed a blank space on a map of Australia. He assumed this was 'an area in which to grow'. Charles Chalmers left Mungindi in 1921 with his wife Cora and three children, 300 sheep, 4 cattle, and 13 horses.

Against the advice of all his friends and also from people he met on the way, Chalmers arrived at Boulia in late 1921. He found the area ravaged by drought. Rain fell by mid-1923 and the Chalmers family moved on toward their new home. Chance showers helped them through a generally water-less land. On arrival their first task was to find permanent water and to build a home.

They named their property McDonald Downs after their two sons and undaunted by the harshness of the land began to live their dream. Charles and Cora had a different outlook to many pastoralists of their time. They insisted their family be generous to the 'Natives'. The family were all fluent in the local Alyawarra language, respecting their customs and beliefs.

Their son Mac took over management of the station and married Rose Agars in 1940. The couple raised six children and the second youngest, Charlie went on to manage the property. In 2011 Charlie Chalmers signed a conservation covenant creating the Mac and Rose Chalmers Conservation Reserve. The 474 hectare reserve encompasses Tower Rock, his mother's favourite picnic area and the final resting place of his parents Mac and Rose. Camping permitted.

32. Arlparra Store

Arlparra Store is on an area of Aboriginal Land formerly known as Utopia Station. Fuel and food are available weekdays from 9 am to 5 pm and Saturday from 9 am to 12 noon. Emergency medical facilities are available at the administrative centre of Urapuntja 20 kilometres west of Arlparra.

33. Sandover Highway

The Sandover Highway is a Northern Territory outback track that forms part of a link between Alice Springs and Mount Isa. No permits are needed to travel on the track or to call at Aboriginal communities that advertise services such as fuel and food. Track conditions can vary considerably as there is 750 kilometres of dry weather road linking the Stuart Highway and the Barkly Highway.

Even during dry conditions the tracks can be difficult due to large sections of heavy bulldust. A 4WD vehicle is highly recommended when travelling any part of these tracks. Travellers on the Binns Track only use a short section of the Sandover Highway. Fuel is available at Arlparra Store 35 kilometres west of the Binns Track along the Sandover Highway.

34. Ammaroo

Ammaroo Station is a fully operational 3000 square kilometre pastoral property running Droughtmaster cattle. The Binns Track passes through the northern part of Ammaroo.

Boxhole Meteorite Crater

MAP 4
NT
SA
N
MERIDIAN
Sandover Highway to Murray Downs turn off 127 km
135ºE
BINNS
TRACK
75
127
ELKEDRA
George
59
Ck
Creek
Trew
MURRAY DOWNS
AMMAROO
OORATIPPRA
24
Atcherie
Ampilatwatja (Aherrenge)
Honeymoon Bore
SANDOVER
95
Arganara Bore
14
HWY
Ck
Antarrengenge
ALAYAWARRA ABORIGINAL LAND TRUST
33
Ammaroo
34
floodout
Sandover
River
HIGHWAY
28
This is a sandy narrow single vehicle track from Derry Downs to Irultja and slightly wider through to Sandover Highway.
No 8 Bore
Urapuntja
18
Corella Bore
18
Atheleye
Irultja
22ºS
14
17
32
ANGARAPA ABORIGINAL LAND TRUST
31
River
DERRY DOWNS
Arlparra Store
Derry Downs
River
SANDOVER
35
Sandover
No access via Derry Downs. Take care at creek crossings due to very soft sand.
Bundey
Utopia Community
ARAPUNYA
Ledan Peak 558 m
42
Creek
Old MacDonald Downs
Arapunga
Arapunya
River
150
DELMORE DOWNS
MacDonald Downs
31
TRACK
Ck
Bundey
Ooratippra
Waite River
Delmore Downs
Tower Rock 554 m
Mt Ultim 612 m
DULCIE RANGE
Mac & Rose Chalmers CR
Delny
MACDONALD DOWNS
22
30
Boxhole Meteorite Crater
ALCOOTA
River
Mount Swan
Dneiper
Dulcie Ranges National Park
(NO public access)
DELNY
7
HUCKITTA
Ck
Bundey
Waite
BINNS
30
DNEIPER
Mt Sainthill 546 m
Engenala
Table Hill 613 m
River
Entire Point 516 m
Marshall
River
Alcoota
Conical Hill 588 m
Plenty
Ck
Prossers Bore
Ongeva
MT RIDDOCK
28
Huckitta
HIGHWAY
25
Jinka
PLENTY
12
Harts Range Police Station
27
Entire
Mount Eaglebeak
Tent Hill 492 m
38
Plenty Highway to Mud Tank Bore 93 km
42
22
Atitjera
23ºS
93
23
Ck
Mount Riddock
51
Harts Range Fossicking Area
Mt Mary 909 m
Fossicking Area

35. Hatches Creek

Prospectors have been searching for gold in the Davenport Ranges since the 1890s but it was Wolframite (Tungsten ore) found in 1914 that caused the first mining boom in this area. Wolfram, used in the hardening of steel and especially used in armaments, was suddenly in high demand during WWI. Mining almost ceased until 1938 when 200 men were working in this area. Good prices during WWII and the Korean War caused another boom that continued until the mid-1960s.

Mining at Hatches Creek was extremely difficult. Droughts and high temperatures caused water shortages. Mining was done by hand. Supplies and tungsten ore were transported by camel train 1,100 kilometres to and from Oodnadatta. Poor living conditions and falling prices finally caused mining to cease by 1968. WWII and the Korean war provided the last two bursts of activity at Hatches Creek. Gold was found in 1898 near Kurundi but it was not profitable on a large scale.

36. Police Station Waterhole

Permanent water has meant that the area known as Old Police Station Waterhole has always been a focus for human activity. The Warumungu, Alyawarre and Kaytetye people used it for thousands of years. Small flint quarries and artefacts relating to occupancy of the land can still be found.

In 1889 Frew River and Elkedra Stations were settled but abandoned a few years later due to poor cattle prices and droughts. By 1920 the area was once again running cattle and a warden was required at Hatches Creek so a police station was built by the waterhole. However, the police presence could not be sustained and the station closed within a few years. Camping available. Small fee applies. More information www.parksandwildlife.nt.gov.au

37. Kurundi Homestead

Kurundi is a large cattle station of about 3300 square kilometres with a long history of association with the Lewis family of South Australia. James Lewis accompanied Charles Sturt on his harrowing Expedition of 1844 into Central Australia. James and his brother John rode the 'Pony Express' on the Overland Telegraph Line in 1872.

A waterhole on Kurundi is named Jim Lewis Waterhole after the son of James Lewis.

38. Devils Marbles (Karlu Karlu)

The name Karlu Karlu roughly means 'big round rocks' or 'lots of rocks' and is traditional country for the Warumungu, Kaytetye, Alawarra and Walpiri people. Almost the entire area of the conservation reserve is registered as a sacred site and is managed by the traditional owners together with the Parks and Wildlife Commission of the Northern Territory. See photo next page.

This remarkable confusion of rocks is where Ralph Milner lost about 3000 sheep after they ate poison bush. This happened in 1871 while his party was walking the first mob of sheep across Australia from Port Augusta to Darwin. In 1953 one of the boulders was removed and placed on Reverend John Flynn's grave at the foot of Mt Gillen west of Alice Springs. In 1999 this boulder was returned to its sacred site at Karlu Karlu. In a gesture of reconciliation a similar rock was selected by the Arrente people from a sacred site near Alice Springs and now marks the grave of John and Jean Flynn.

39. Bonney Well

John McDouall Stuart named Bonney Creek in 1860 during his first attempt to cross Australia. A party overlanding cattle and sheep into the Northern Territory sank a shallow well in early 1879 and it is likely that a party of well sinkers under contract to the Post Master General's Department enlarged the well to a depth of about 10 metres. A stone tank stand, headframe and whip were added ten years later and continued to be used by travelers and stock alike until the 1930s when a windmill was built nearby.

A staging camp was set up at Bonney Well during WWII and much of the infrastructure was destroyed during the war. Restoration was commissioned by the National Trust in 1984 and declared a Heritage place in 1996. Bonney Well is one of only three remaining wells on the North-South Stock Route with stone dumps intact.

Bonney Creek Waterhole

Old Police Station ruins

Devils Marbles (see number 38 on Map 5)

40. Tennant Creek

The township takes its name from a nearby creek named by John McDouall Stuart in 1860 after his associate John Tennant of Port Lincoln. A Telegraph Repeater Station was built at Tennant Creek in 1870 as part of the Overland Telegraph Line linking Australia with Europe. (The original telegraph station still exists several kilometres north of the town and is well worth a visit.) Gold was discovered in 1926 but the gold rush did not occur until 1932 when about 600 miners converged on the area and a small town quickly developed. Mining has not been easy due to isolation, drought and the need to crush ironstone in which the gold is found. However, mining is still Tennant Creek's most important industry with more than 210 tonnes of gold produced in the area during the last 80 years. Manganese and copper are also mined.

Tennant Creek today is the regional hub of the Barkly Region and serves the needs of station people, pastoralists and mining companies.

Mary Ann Dam, to the north of Tennant Creek, is a shady, recreational area with showers and toilets.

41. Three Ways

North of Tennant Creek the intersection of the Stuart and Barkly Highways is known as Three Ways. Here an imposing structure stands in memory of the legendary achievements of John Flynn, founder of the Royal Flying Doctor Service. Flynn had a vision of providing a 'Mantle of Safety' over all of the isolated areas of Australia. This vision became the World's first Flying Doctor Service which still operates along similar lines to Flynn's original vision but now operates with 21st Century technology.

42. Attack Creek Historical Reserve

The reserve is a memorial to explorer John McDouall Stuart who reached this point in 1860 while trying to find a suitable track across Australia. Stuart, together with William Kekwick and Benjamin Head were met by hostile Aborigines and forced to return to Adelaide. Stuart successfully crossed Australia in 1861 using Attack Creek as a campsite and reliable water source.

In 1871 Ralph Milner was overlanding sheep along Stuart's track bound for Darwin and while shepherding stock at Attack Creek his brother John was killed by an Aborigine who crept up behind him while he was resting. John Milner is buried at Stuart's campsite several kilometres east of the Highway.

43. Renner Springs

Renner Springs owes its name to Dr Renner who attended to the medical needs of workers on the Overland Telegraph Line. It is believed that Renner was the first European to notice birds congregating in an area that when investigated proved to be a reliable water source.

Lubra's Lookout, a flat top rock 4km south of Renner Springs, was so named after the Aboriginal women who used it as a viewing point to observe the return of their men from hunting. Most traveller's needs are available at Renner Springs.

The memorial to John McDouall Stuart at Attack Creek

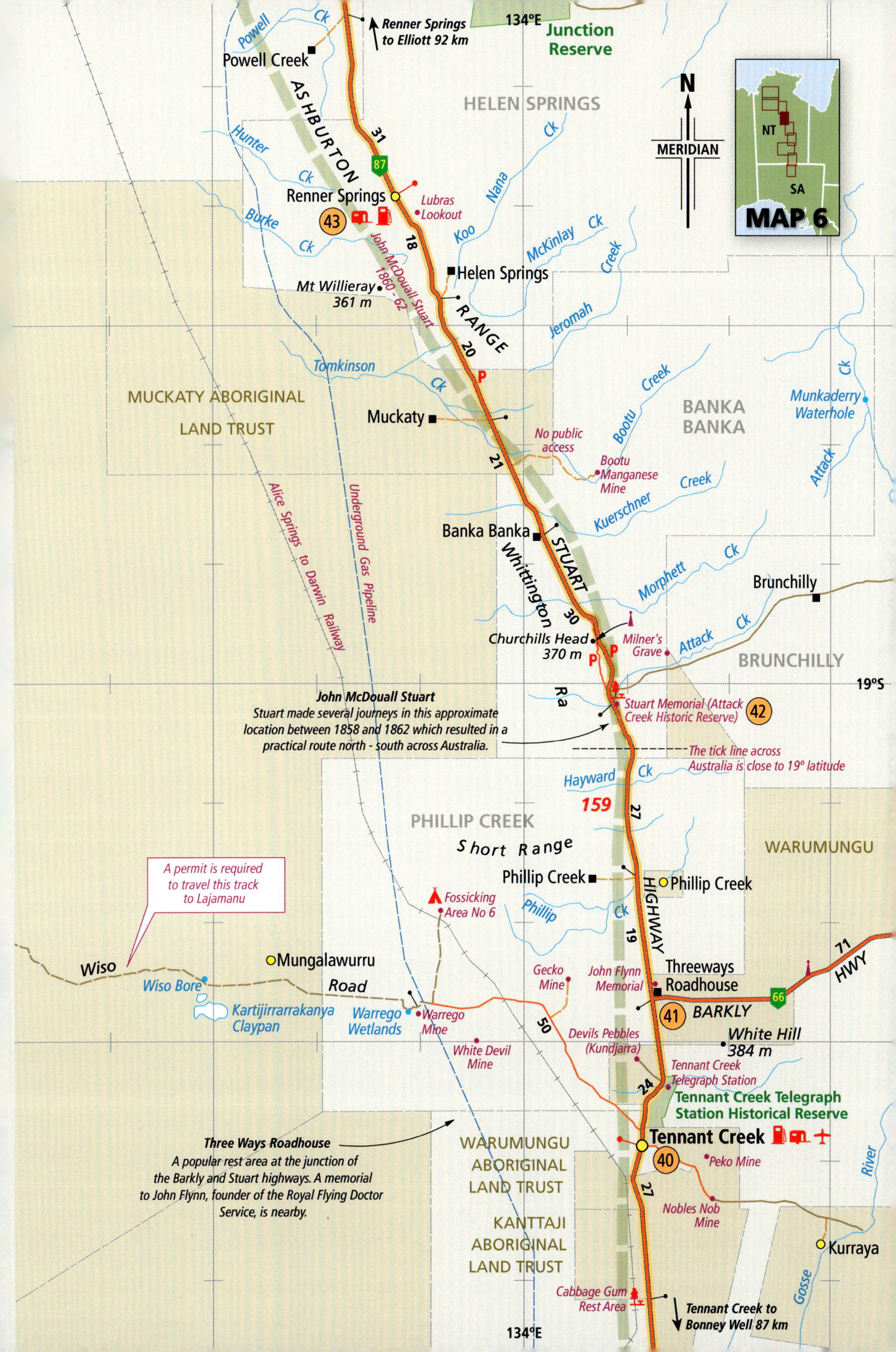

MAP 6
NT
SA
N
MERIDIAN
134°E
Renner Springs to Elliott 92 km
Junction Reserve
Powell Creek
Powell Ck
HELEN SPRINGS
ASHBURTON
RANGE
Hunter Ck
Burke Ck
Renner Springs
Lubras Lookout
43
Nana Ck
Koo
McKinlay Ck
Creek
Helen Springs
Mt Willieray 361 m
John McDouall Stuart 1860 - 62
Jeromah
Tomkinson Ck
MUCKATY ABORIGINAL LAND TRUST
Muckaty
No public access
Bootu Creek
Bootu Manganese Mine
BANKA BANKA
Munkaderry Waterhole
Attack Ck
Kuerschner Creek
Banka Banka
Whittington
STUART
Alice Springs to Darwin Railway
Underground Gas Pipeline
Morphett Ck
Brunchilly
BRUNCHILLY
Churchills Head 370 m
Milner's Grave
Attack Ck
19°S
Ra
John McDouall Stuart
Stuart made several journeys in this approximate location between 1858 and 1862 which resulted in a practical route north - south across Australia.
Stuart Memorial (Attack Creek Historic Reserve)
42
The tick line across Australia is close to 19° latitude
Hayward Ck
159
PHILLIP CREEK
Short Range
WARUMUNGU
Phillip Creek
Phillip Creek
HIGHWAY
A permit is required to travel this track to Lajamanu
Fossicking Area No 6
Phillip Ck
Wiso
Mungalawurru
Road
Wiso Bore
Kartijirrarrakanya Claypan
Warrego Wetlands
Warrego Mine
Gecko Mine
John Flynn Memorial
Threeways Roadhouse
71 HWY
66
41
BARKLY
White Devil Mine
Devils Pebbles (Kundjarra)
White Hill 384 m
Tennant Creek Telegraph Station
Tennant Creek Telegraph Station Historical Reserve
Three Ways Roadhouse
A popular rest area at the junction of the Barkly and Stuart highways. A memorial to John Flynn, founder of the Royal Flying Doctor Service, is nearby.
WARUMUNGU ABORIGINAL LAND TRUST
Tennant Creek
40
Peko Mine
River
Nobles Nob Mine
KANTTAJI ABORIGINAL LAND TRUST
Kurraya
Gosse
Cabbage Gum Rest Area
Tennant Creek to Bonney Well 87 km
134°E

44. Powell Creek Telegraph Station

The Powell Creek Telegraph Station was built along the Overland Telegraph Line while it was being constructed during 1871-72. Remains of the site are fragile and are not open to the public.

Between Powell Creek and Elliot it is possible to get a glimpse of Lake Woods about 10 kilometres west of the Stuart Highway. Another feature in this area worth the short drive is the Barkly Tablelands which can be seen about ten kilometres east along the Barkly Stock Route. Huge black-soil plains covered with waving Mitchell grass caused problems for drovers bringing cattle over from the Kimberley to eastern markets. Although Mitchell Grass is good feed, the scarcity of trees caused problems for cooks trying to provide meals and the lack of surface water made droving cattle very difficult. Underground water and road transport has made cattle handling much easier on the Barkly Tableland.

45. Elliot

Elliot is a relatively modern township named after Captain R D (Snow) Elliot MBE who was responsible for the operation of the WWII Staging Camp at Newcastle Waters No 8 Bore. Captain Elliot's superiors were so impressed with the neatness and efficiency of the camp that it became known as Elliot's camp. A small town with reasonable services available.

Longreach Waterhole is a protected area managed by the Northern Territory Parks and Wildlife service. It is a popular bush-camping area for tourists but with few facilities.

46. Newcastle Waters

A stretch of semi-permanent waterholes was named Newcastle Waters in 1861 by explorer John McDouall Stuart after the Duke of Newcastle, Secretary for the Colonies. Newcastle Waters Station was established by Dr WJ Browne who also established Springvale Station near Katherine. Browne sold to John Lewis in 1895 and the land was held by the Lewis family for the next 50 years. (See No 30, Kurundi Station). Although stock from the north and west had been walked along the stock-routes through Newcastle Waters since the late 1800s the township was not established until 1930. It operated as a focal point for drovers moving back and forth along the stock routes for the next 30 years. Road transport quickly replaced on-the-hoof droving and by 1962 the town was almost deserted.

47. Overland Telegraph Memorial

This memorial is about 2 kilometres east of the actual spot where the northern and southern sections of the Overland Telegraph Line were joined. Construction of the line started in September 1870, under the direction of Charles Todd. Appalling conditions during the wet season hindered completion of the northern section and completion was seven months late when Robert Patterson described joining of the Overland Telegraph Line on July 22, 1872.

"Half the party seized hold of me and the wire, and the other half of the other end, and stretched with all might and main to bring the two ends together. All our force could not do this. I then attached some binding wire to one end. The moment I brought it to the other end the current passed through my body from all the batteries on the line. I had to yell and let go. Next time I proceeded more cautiously, and used my handkerchief to seize the wire. In about five minutes I had the joint made complete, and Adelaide was in communication with Port Darwin. It would have been with England had not the (overseas) cable broken down".

Overland Telegraph Memorial at Frews Ponds

It took less than two years to complete 3,200 kilometres of telegraph line through country where few Europeans had ever travelled. A section of 52 poles are preserved intact near Frews Ponds.

48. Dunmurra

An Overland Telegraph linesman disappeared in this locality in 1871. About 1930 Noel Healy found a skeleton while setting up a cattle station. The skeleton was identified as Dan O'Mara, the missing linesman. Attempts by Aborigines to pronounce Dan O'Mara sounded like Dunmarra so that is what Healy called his station. Several years later Healy built a store beside the track connecting Alice Springs with Darwin.

The lagoon across the road from the Dunmurra Roadhouse was named after Ralph Milner who overlanded about 3,000 sheep from the south heading toward Darwin. Milner used this lagoon on his way north in 1871.

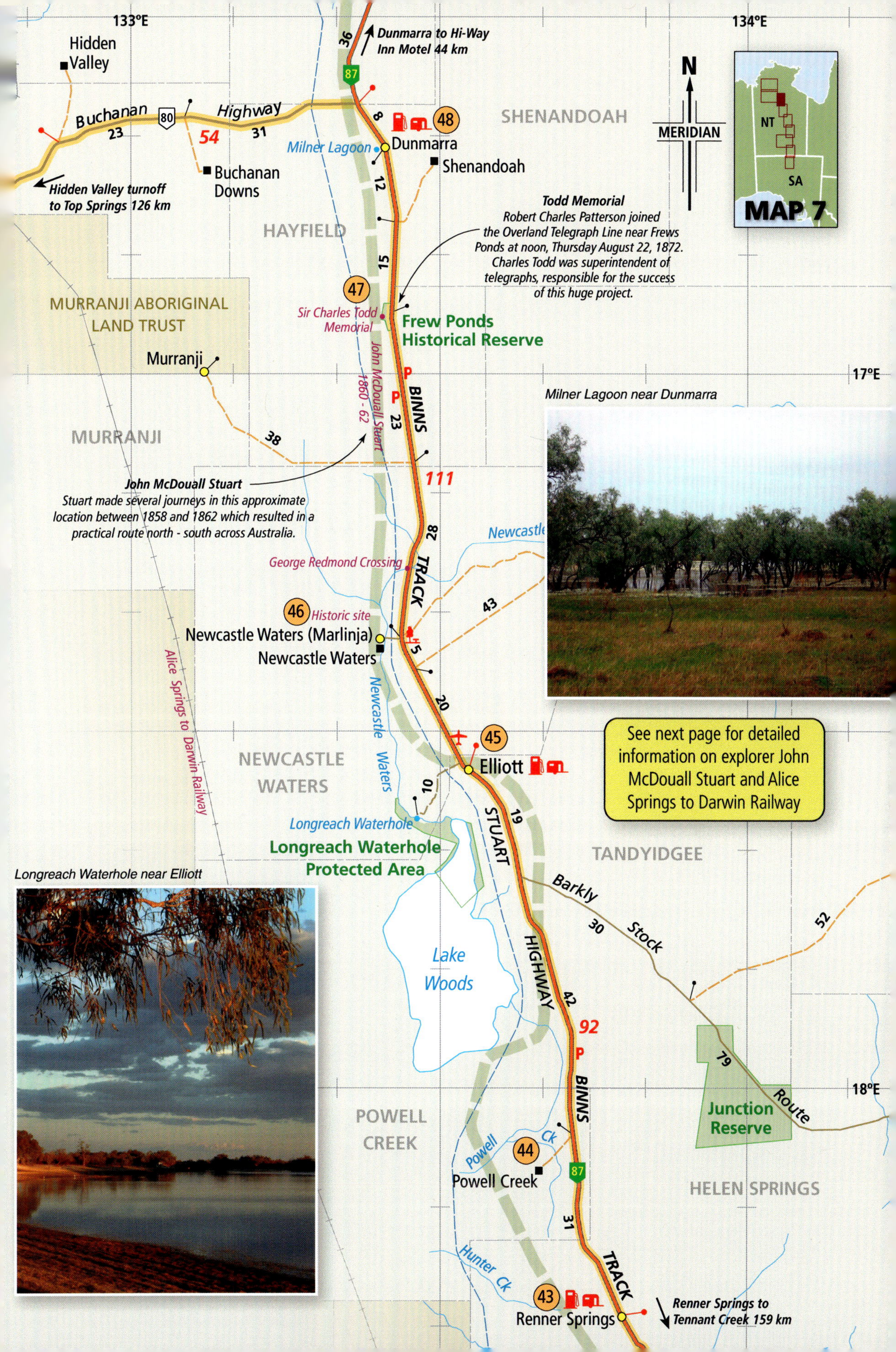

See next page for detailed information on explorer John McDouall Stuart and Alice Springs to Darwin Railway

Milner Lagoon near Dunmarra

Longreach Waterhole near Elliott

John McDouall Stuart

Stuart dominated Australian exploration in the 1850s to 1860s. Other explorers had been into and even north of the Flinders Ranges, but it was Stuart who made the most impact on Australian history in this area. (The Burke and Wills expedition of 1860-61 also opened up a huge area of Australia and was technically the first expedition to cross the country from south to north. However, their route was almost 400 kilometres to the east.)

Stuart's attempts, financed by James and John Chambers, and William Finke were successful, especially when compared with the size and cost of the Burke and Wills expedition. Stuart, with two other men and thirteen horses, left Stuart Creek in 1860, on the first of three almost continual treks across Australia. It was on this trip that Stuart became the first non-Aboriginal to visit the centre of Australia. He named the location Central Mt Sturt, which was soon changed to Central Mt Stuart, in his honour.

As he pushed northwards, on what later became the route of the Overland Telegraph Line, Stuart named Peake Creek, the Neales River, Mt Dutton, Mt O'Halloran, the Stevenson and Finke Rivers. Stuart's party was forced to return after conflict with Aborigines at Attack Creek, just north of Tennant Creek. In 1861 he again set out determined to cross the continent, but was forced to return after failing to find water north of Newcastle Waters, only 160 kilometres north of Attack Creek.

Stuart finally did cross Australia and on July 24, 1862, he was standing on the coast east of present-day Darwin. By the time he returned to Adelaide in December, 1862, he had travelled about 16,000 kilometres in three trips through some of the harshest country in the world. During those trips he spent a total of only three months refitting time in Adelaide. This enormous effort ruined his health and almost certainly contributed to his early death.

First Stock to Cross Australia 1870-72

Ralph Milner, his brother John and twelve men left Pt Augusta in September 1870 with 4300 sheep, 160 horses, 17 bullocks, 150 goats and 20 dogs bound for Port Darwin. This was their second attempt after becoming stranded north of Marree for seven years. They expected to travel almost 5000 kilometres through unknown country with scarce feed and usable water. A good season helped them through to the Finke River where they met deep flood waters. After several days they were able to encourage the stock to swim through the flowing water. The party camped further north at Owen Springs for shearing and lambing.

Ralph Milner and his party eventually moved northwards with an increased mob of about 7000 sheep and after a few weeks reached the Devil's Marbles. Here 3000 sheep died after feeding on shrubs found to be poisonous. They quickly moved on and rested at Attack Creek, previously named by Stuart during his 1860 exploration. John Milner was sitting by a tree while minding sheep when an Aborigine crept up attacked him with a club. John Milner is buried at the edge of Attack Creek.

A sad party moved on to the Roper River and discovered Telegraph Linesmen starving as the wet season had held up supplies. Ralph Milner sold most of his sheep to the Linesmen during the months they were stranded here. He also explored a route to the mouth of the Roper River.

When the country dried fit for travel Milner's party together with the remaining stock finally reached Port Darwin in June 1872. They were not only the first with stock to cross Australia they also the first to drive two spring carts, two bullock drays and one large horse wagon across the continent.

Waterhole on Attack Creek near Stuart's Camp and John Milner's Grave

The Central Australian Railway

The concept of this railway was to link Palmerston (now Darwin) with Adelaide, although it may have started from pressure by farmers to serve northern areas of South Australia for wheat growing. The South Australian Government built the line from Palmerston to Pine Creek by 1889 and from Pt Augusta to Oodnadatta by January, 1890. In 1911 South Australia relinquished its claim to the Northern Territory due to problems governing and financing the remote area. Part of the agreement to let the new Federal Government take over the Northern Territory was that a rail line was to be built connecting Oodnadatta to Pine Creek. However, freight was carried into Central Australia from Oodnadatta by camel train for many years until August, 1929 when the line to Alice Springs was completed. It was anticipated that the North Australia Railway would be built south to Daly Waters but because Australia was entering the depression years money was not available and it was decided to terminate at Birdum in September 1929.

The line was barely viable for the years leading up to the Second World War (WWII) when the terminus was shifted to Larrimah due to the area around Birdum being low-lying and unsuitable for the thousands of tonnes of freight and passengers it was expected to carry during the war. Both north and south rail lines and the vast trucking convoys between Alice Springs and Larrimah were part of the largest Allied land-based transport operation of WWII.

Following the war there were periods of fluctuating fortunes as mining flourished and waned until finally the last train on the northern line arrived in Darwin on the 30th June 1976.

The Ghan was the name of the train that operated in the south where water was one of the main basic needs when choosing an alignment. This was also the case with the telegraph, so it is not surprising they took similar routes. Eventually the telegraph line was moved to the railway line, making repairs easier. Water also caused the ultimate closure of the railway, as flash floods caused great damage and maintenance was very expensive. On some rivers low-level bridges proved to be superior to high-level bridges as debris from floods tended to flow over low-level causeways instead of building up against bridge-work causing damage to high-level bridges. Both types were built on the Finke River but it was found to be more efficient to simply rebuild the line in the river-bed each time it washed away.

Diesel locomotives replaced steam engines in 1954 and many water points then fell into disrepair. The original Ghan train ran for the last time in 1980 and an exhibit can now be seen at the Road Transport Hall of Fame in Alice Springs.

In October 1980 a new standard gauge railway was opened from Tarcoola in South Australia to Alice Springs. The position of the new line was not influenced by a need for water or fuel so it was able to be sited on high ridges running most of the way to Alice Springs. This has overcome many flooding problems that plagued the old line through Oodnadatta.

Construction of the final link between Alice Springs and Darwin started in July 2001 and was completed in December 2003. The first freight train into Darwin arrived in mid-January 2004 and the first passenger train about two weeks later, completing the Federal government's agreement with South Australia made more than 80 years earlier.

The Algebuckina Bridge is the longest in South Australia

49. No 11 Bore, Murranji Track

The first use of the Murranji Track by Europeans most likely happened during the late 1880s. The 1890s were very dry and few cattle travelled the stock routes. However, during the next 20 years thousands of cattle were walked across what was one of the worst stock routes in Australia. The few waterholes on the track were unreliable making dry-staging of cattle a perilous task.

An unknown number of men and cattle died along the Murranji Track. In 1924 a major Government upgrade of the Murranji took place when bores and tanks were installed making the movement of stock more reliable. Bulldozers were also used to clear a wide path through the thickest of the bush.

Cattle along the Murranji Track

50. Top Springs

The original Top Springs homestead was located near and possibly named after a nearby waterhole about nine kilometres south east of the present roadhouse. Top Springs was regarded as the start of the Murranji Stock Route first explored by Nat Buchanan and Sam Croker in 1887.

The Murranji ran from Top Springs to Newcastle Waters to join the Barkly Stock Route into Queensland. This track was many hundreds of kilometres shorter than the previous stock route that followed the Gulf Track much further to the north.

The Murranji Stock Route was a most difficult track with poor water supply, dense bullwaddy forests and stony ground noted for being 'drummy'. Cattle became very nervous from the sound of drummy ground, rushed for limited water and became injured by dangerous trees.

The stock route became vitally important during WW II but quickly lapsed into disuse after the introduction of road trains during the early 1960s. What remains of the stock route runs adjacent to the

Fording the Victoria River at Dashwood Crossing along the Buchanan Highway east of Victoria River Downs

Buchanan Highway from Top Springs to the Alice Springs railway where it turns south east toward Newcastle Waters. Contact Top Springs Roadhouse on (08) 8975 0767.

51. Victoria River Downs (VRD)

VRD was originally established in 1880 by Charles Fisher and Maurice Lyons who stocked the property with 20,000 head of cattle that had been overlanded from Queensland by Nat Buchanan. At that time it was the world's largest pastoral property with an area of 41,000 square kilometres.

By 1894 VRD carried in excess of 30,000 head of cattle and about 500 horses. Cattle were being shipped to Batavia (Indonesia) and Singapore. However, due to its size VRD was difficult to run and several syndicates found it difficult to make profits. In 1900 two of the largest cattle men of the time, Sydney Kidman and Isadore Emanuel headed a syndicate that purchased VRD. This was one of the few companies to successfully run and make profits from VRD during its early years.

By 1923 the size of the property was reduced to about 33,929 square kilometres still the largest property

Victoria River Downs station

The large boab tree with dates carved by Augustus Gregory's North Australia Expedition party in 1855-56.

in the Northern Territory at the time. Parts of the property have since been excised due to Government Regulations leaving an area of about 12,000 square kilometres. VRD has been operating for over 100 years and is currently owned by Heytesbury Pty Ltd. The station is served by the Victoria River Downs Airport, also owned by Heytesbury.

52. Judbarra/Gregory National Park

This park covers an area of around 13,000 square kilometres and is named after explorer Augustus C Gregory who led the North Australia Expedition in 1855-56. A living monument to this expedition is Gregory's Tree, a large boab tree with the dates of arrival and departure of the explorers cut into it. The Park features spectacular range and gorge scenery and significant traces of Aboriginal culture, European exploration and pastoral history.

53. Humbert River Station

Although a Pastoral Permit was issued for Humbert River in 1903 little use was made of it until Charlie Schultz purchased the Grazing Licence in 1919. Fat cattle were walked to the Wyndham meatworks or overland to Queensland via the Murranji and Barkly Stock Routes. Humbert River is now part of the Consolidated Pastoral Company which operates more than 20 cattle stations across Australia.

54. Bullita Outstation

This section of Judbarra/Gregory National Park was an outstation for the Durack family who were pioneers in the cattle industry. The Duracks established several huge cattle stations in western Queensland then moved to the Kimberley and established more stations during the 1880s.

The old Bullita homestead still stands and the name of one of the Duracks is carved into a nearby boab tree. Land from Victoria River Downs, Humbert River, Delamere, Auvergne, and Innesvale Stations was also excised to create Gregory National Park.

55. Jasper Gorge

An Aboriginal Dreaming Place where dreaming sites can still be seen as paintings, rocks and marks on the cliff face. For Europeans it is a place of conflict where teamsters were besieged and killed, boulders rolled down on passing herds and supplies stolen from wagons trapped in the gorge. Augustus Gregory was the first European to explore this gorge that passed through a range of hills he previously named Jasper Range.

The gorge was the only way through Jasper Range and was the only access for people from Victoria River Downs to the depot on the Victoria River near Timber Creek. Conflict continued in Jasper Gorge well into the 20th Century and one report even suggests that it was still possible to request a police escort through Jasper Gorge as late as 1950.

Jasper Gorge waterhole

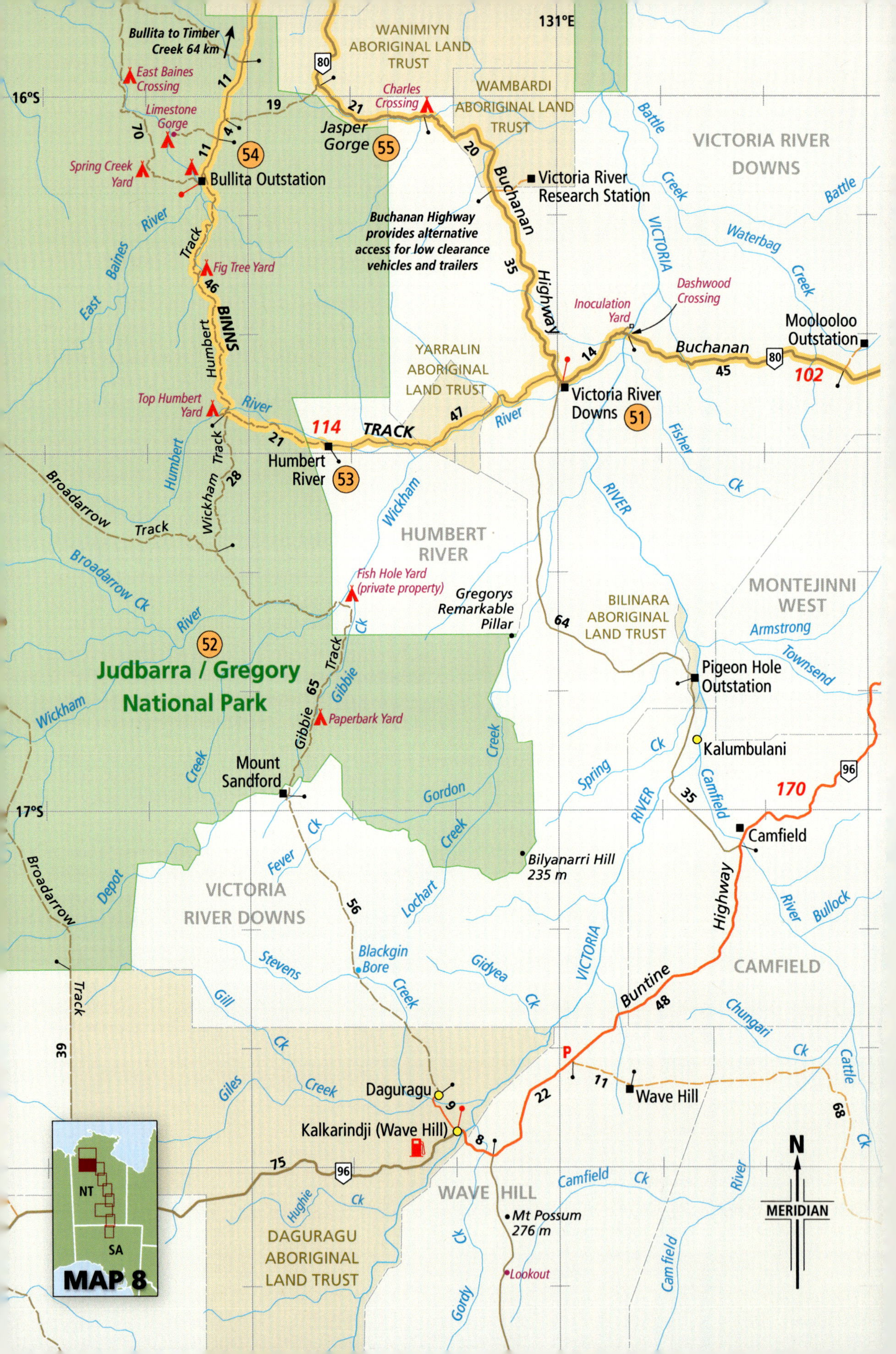
Bullita to Timber Creek 64 km
East Baines Crossing
Limestone Gorge
Spring Creek Yard
Bullita Outstation
54
WANIMIYN ABORIGINAL LAND TRUST
80
Charles Crossing
Jasper Gorge
55
131°E
16°S
WAMBARDI ABORIGINAL LAND TRUST
VICTORIA RIVER DOWNS
Victoria River Research Station
Buchanan Highway provides alternative access for low clearance vehicles and trailers
Battle Creek
Waterbag Creek
Dashwood Crossing
Inoculation Yard
Moolooloo Outstation
Buchanan
102
Fig Tree Yard
East Baines River
Track
BINNS
Humbert
YARRALIN ABORIGINAL LAND TRUST
Victoria River Downs
51
Top Humbert Yard
River
114
TRACK
Humbert River
53
Broadarrow Track
Wickham Track
Fisher Ck
HUMBERT RIVER
RIVER
Broadarrow Ck
Fish Hole Yard (private property)
Gregorys Remarkable Pillar
MONTEJINNI WEST
BILINARA ABORIGINAL LAND TRUST
Armstrong
Townsend
Pigeon Hole Outstation
52
Judbarra / Gregory National Park
Gibbie Track
Paperbark Yard
Kalumbulani
Mount Sandford
Gordon Creek
Spring Ck
Camfield
17°S
170
96
Camfield
Bilyanarri Hill 235 m
Fever Ck
Depot
Lochart
VICTORIA RIVER DOWNS
Highway
Bullock
Blackgin Bore
Stevens
Gidyea Ck
VICTORIA
CAMFIELD
Gill Ck
Creek
Buntine
Chungari Ck
Giles Creek
Daguragu
Wave Hill
Cattle Ck
Kalkarindji (Wave Hill)
WAVE HILL
Camfield Ck
River
N
MERIDIAN
Hughie Ck
Mt Possum 276 m
DAGURAGU ABORIGINAL LAND TRUST
Lookout
Gordy
Camfield
NT
SA
MAP 8

Waterhole on the East Baines River near Bullita Outstation

A large boab tree near Bullita Outstation

56. Timber Creek

In 1855, A C Gregory and a party of 19 men reached the mouth of the Victoria River in a boat called the Tom Tough. They sailed up-river to land near the present town of Timber Creek and established a base camp. Gregory named a nearby stream Timber Creek while searching for timber to repair his boat. Gregory marked a large boab tree near the original campsite about 15 kilometres from the present town. A police station was built in 1898, and as river traffic increased to serve pastoral properties being established in the area a supply depot was established in 1911.

During WWII growing concerns over a Japanese invasion of northern Australia led to the formation of the 2/1st North Australia Observer Unit. This unit was given the nickname 'Nackeroos' and was a highly mobile reconnaissance unit guided by local Aborigines. Their role was to report any enemy landings on isolated areas of the coastline. The Nackeroos were recognised in 1998 when a memorial was constructed near the town. Timber Creek was proclaimed a town on 20 June 1975.

In 1996, the Department of Defence purchased Bradshaw Station, a large cattle property north west of Timber Creek. This land is now the Bradshaw Field Training Area, an area of 8700 square kilometres used for 'live-fire' training. In 2002 the 270m long Bradshaw Bridge opened providing road access to the training area from the Victoria Highway at Timber Creek. A range of services and accommodation is available.

57. Victoria River Roadhouse

The roadhouse provides for an increasing number of travellers on the Victoria Highway. Traffic increased dramatically following completion of the Ord River Diversion Dam at Kununurra in Western Australia in 1963. Construction of the 'new' road bridge was completed in 1970 and sealing of the Victoria Highway in 1974.

58. Katherine

Ludwig Leichhardt was the first European to visit the area during his 1844 expedition to Port Essington when he crossed the headwaters of the Katherine River. However, it was not until 1862 that the river was named Catherine, by John McDouall Stuart, after the second daughter of his benefactor, James Chambers. The name has been misspelled ever since.

Notable visitors to the Katherine and Springvale station during the early years included: Ralph Milner with 4000 sheep in 1872, Alexander Forrest, exploring from Western Australia to Darwin in September 1879 and Frank Hann also in September 1879, with 200 cattle from Queensland. In October 1882 a party led by Adam Johns and Phil Saunders came through from Western Australia prospecting for gold. June 1883 saw the arrival of one of the few female explorers, Mrs Caroline Creaghe, in a party led by Ernest Favenc who explored the area between the Queensland border and the Overland Telegraph Line.

The first town site was located on the banks of the river above the old ford now referred to as Notts Crossing. Although the Katherine Telegraph Station and outbuildings had been in existence since the completion of the line in 1872 and comprised a small village in its own right, there were no substantial commercial buildings until 1888 when the Sportsman's Hotel and Pioneer Cash Store were opened for business. By 1889 the Darwin – Pine Creek railway was complete leaving Katherine residents only 112

Victoria River viewed from Policeman Point Lookout, a few kilometres northwest of Timber Creek

Old Victoria River Crossing, north of Victoria River Roadhouse

kilometres of bush tracks between Katherine and Darwin. The old hotel still stands looking much the same as it did when Mrs Aeneas Gunn, author of *"We of the Never Never"* first crossed the Katherine River at this spot in 1902 on her way to Elsey Station.

In 1911 the South Australian Government realised it could no longer fund the cost of developing the Northern Territory and decided to hand its ownership to the newly-formed Federal Government. One of the conditions of the transfer was an agreement by the Federal Government to purchase the railway line from Port Augusta to Oodnadatta and a commitment to complete the line through to the rail-head at Pine Creek. Although construction was completed from Oodnadatta to Alice Springs in 1928 and from Pine Creek to Katherine in 1917 and Birdum (near Larrimah) about 1930, a complete link to Darwin was not completed until 2004. Prior to WWII Katherine had a population of about 230 people.

A second temporary town site called Emungalan was established in 1917 near the proposed rail head. In 1926 a railway bridge was completed and the residents moved across the river to the present site of Katherine.

Katherine's strategic position was important during WWII, when many military personnel were stationed here. The area was bombed by the Japanese during a raid in 1942. Numerous airstrips were constructed, including the runway now used by the Tindal RAAF Base.

Katherine is an interesting, modern city with a large tourist infrastructure and a population of about 10,000. Visitors often see Katherine as part of a dry landscape and find it difficult to believe that in 1998 flood-water was almost two metres deep in the main street and throughout much of the town.

George Jaensch who worked on the Overland Telegraph Line, together with two other men, are believed to have been the first to navigate a boat along the Katherine River to the coast in 1908.

Nitmiluk National Park. The main attraction is the thirteen spectacular gorges in the Katherine River. A feature is the huge cliff where scenes from the 1950s movie, Jedda, were filmed. Tracks provide a range of walking experiences including Aboriginal art sites and spectacular views. It is not known who the first European was who saw the spectacular gorges but Alfred Giles may well have found them when he was manager of Springvale Station. The Katherine Gorge National Park (now Nitmiluk National Park) was created in 1963.

59. Springvale Station

Alfred Giles, a competent bushman working with an Overland Telegraph Line surveying party, continued to work as a guide for crews and individuals moving up and down the line. Upon completion of the line he decided to overland 5000 sheep to the northern-most telegraph stations. Giles was appointed manager of Springvale Station and again prepared to take a large mob of sheep cattle and horses across Australia.

He crossed the continent seven times during the years he was in the Katherine area. Springvale Station was the second station established in the Northern Territory and the homestead is the oldest still in use. (Undoolya near Alice Springs was the first station in the Northern Territory.)

60. Tindal RAAF Base

Originally known as Carson Airfield, this Royal Australian Airforce base was renamed Tindal after Wing Commander A R Tindal who was killed in action over Darwin during the first Japanese air raid in February 1942. In 1982 the Government commenced building a new RAAF Base at Tindal 17 kilometres south of Katherine. In 1987, personnel began arriving bringing about a large boost to Katherine's population and economy. A squadron of FA 18 Hornets is stationed on the base operated by members of 75 Squadron. Operationally, the inland location offers additional warning time for any attack from seaward.

For peace-time training, the base's remoteness from built up areas means that there is little inconvenience to residents as a result of aircraft activities. Tindal is one of the most important strategic defence bases in Australia. It occupies an area of 122 square kilometres and houses about 900 personnel.

Cutta Cutta and Tindal Caves are found in the Caves Reserve, on the Stuart Highway south of Katherine. These are the only publicly accessible tropical limestone caves in the Northern Territory.

Victoria Highway near Timber Creek showing escarpment landforms typical of the area

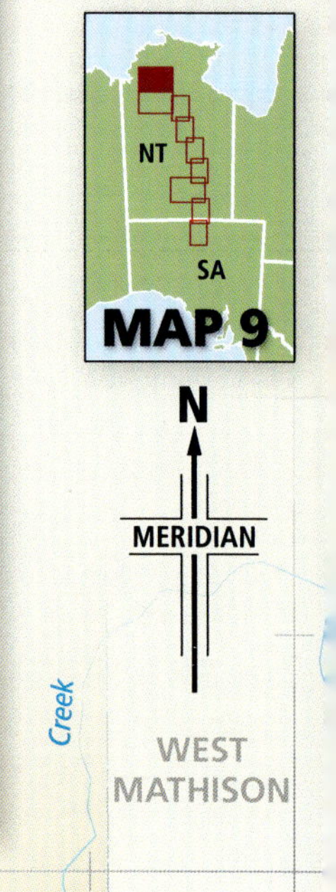

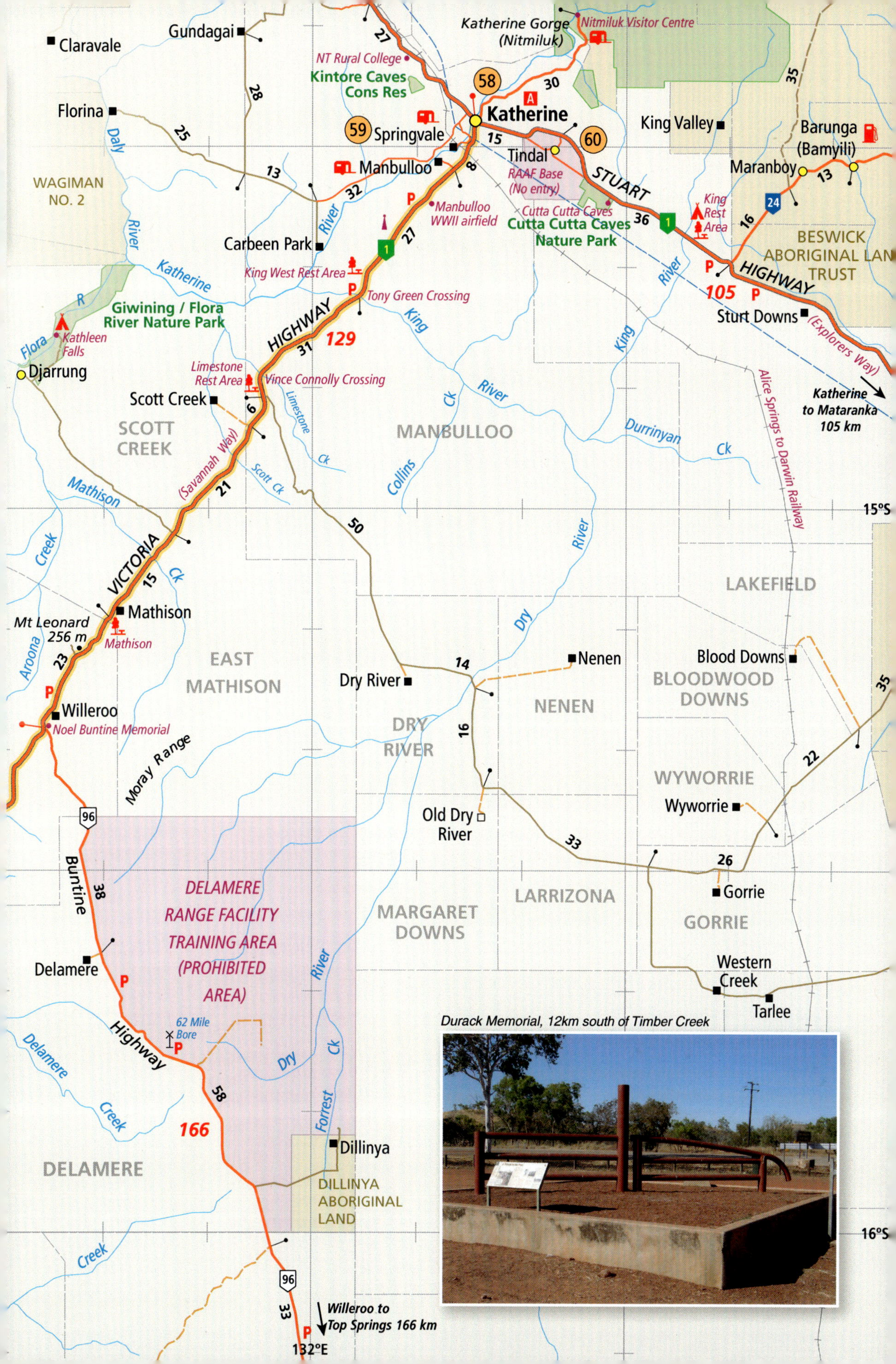

Durack Memorial, 12km south of Timber Creek